COLORING ST. LOUIS
By Andrew Wanko
Art by Rori!

Missouri Historical Society Press
St. Louis
Distributed by University of Chicago Press

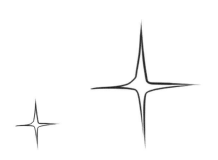

This book is based on the exhibit *Coloring STL*, produced by the Missouri History Museum, August 2022–February 2024.

Exhibit and book graphic elements by Heather Speckhard
Book layout by Lauren Mitchell
Printed and bound in the United States by Modern Litho

-INTRODUCTION-

What is your favorite St. Louis building? Given all of the city's historic landmarks, modern masterpieces, and beautiful neighborhoods, is it even possible to choose just one?

St. Louis is a kaleidoscope of architecture, filled with structures of every age, shape, and size— and in this book, it's your job to color them! Here you'll find more than 30 St. Louis structures, from treasures like the Old Courthouse and the Fox Theatre to the very homes we live in.

So get coloring! We'll provide the history. You provide the imagination.

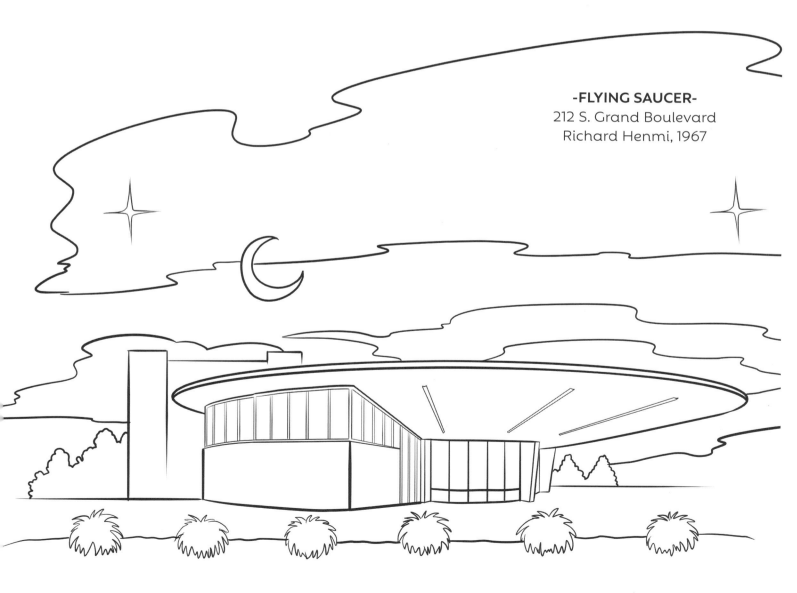

-FLYING SAUCER-
212 S. Grand Boulevard
Richard Henmi, 1967

-FRENCH COLONIAL HOME-
St. Louis riverfront
Various architects, ca. 1760s–1800s

In the fur-trading village of early St. Louis, most homes were built using a French Colonial construction technique called *poteaux en terre* ("posts in earth"). Upright wooden posts formed a home's structural frame, and then rocks or mud were packed in between to create the walls.

These homes typically had two large rooms and a central fireplace that heated both sides.

A wraparound porch provided relief from the summer heat.

St. Louis's French Colonial homes had all disappeared by the 1870s, but the Louis Bolduc House, built in the 1790s, still stands in nearby Ste. Genevieve.

-OLD ST. FERDINAND SHRINE-
1 Rue St. Francois
1819–1888

Rose Philippine Duchesne opened the Academy of the Sacred Heart, a girls' boarding school that accepted French and Native American students, in the tiny hamlet of Florissant in 1819.

St. Ferdinand Church's shingled steeple and stained-glass windows were added in 1883 and gave the church a more Victorian-era feel.

Today, Philippine's 200-year-old boarding house is the oldest portion of Florissant's Old St. Ferdinand Shrine. The next-door St. Ferdinand Church is only two years younger, and today it's the oldest existing church between the Mississippi River and the Rocky Mountains.

In 1988, Mother Rose Philippine Duchesne was canonized by Pope John Paul II as the fourth Catholic saint in United States history.

-OLD COURTHOUSE-
11 N. 4th Street
Various architects, ca. 1826–1864

At 192 feet, the Old Courthouse was Missouri's tallest structure from 1864 to 1894, when it was surpassed by Union Station.

The cast-iron and copper dome weighs an estimated 128 tons.

It took more than a half dozen architects to finish the building over four decades.

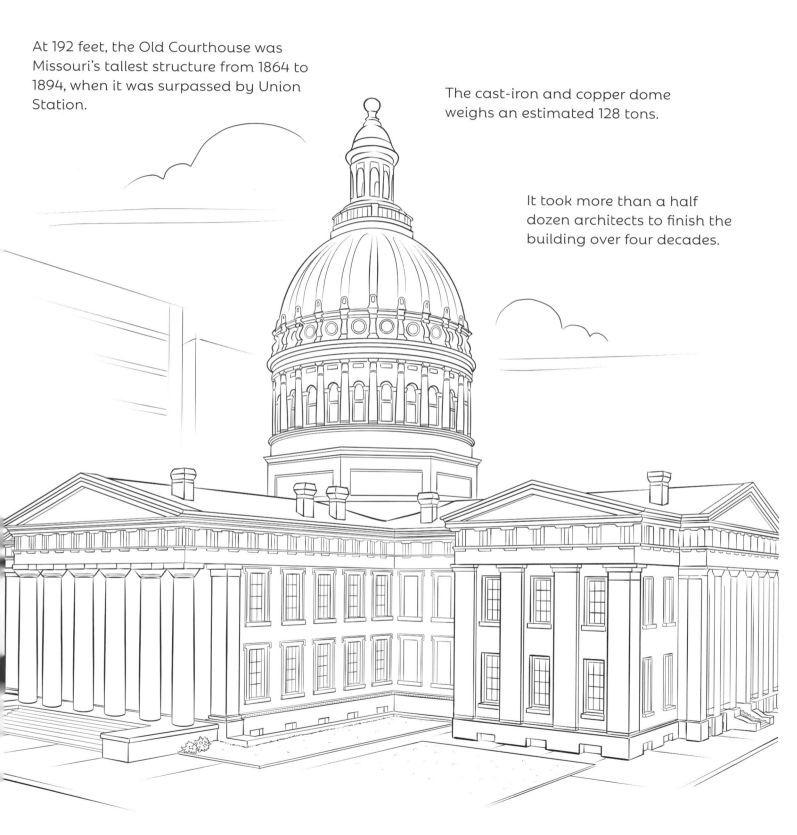

Enslaved persons Dred and Harriet Scott first sued for their freedom here in 1846.

-TOWER GROVE HOUSE-
Missouri Botanical Garden
George I. Barnett, 1849

When wealthy hardware merchant Henry Shaw built his rural retreat named "Tower Grove," it sat amid the rolling countryside far from the urban density of St. Louis.

A campanile is a central tower—a defining feature of the Italianate-style home.

Shaw opened his home's gardens to the public as the Missouri Botanical Garden in 1859.

The house predates Tower Grove Park by 20 years and gave the park its name.

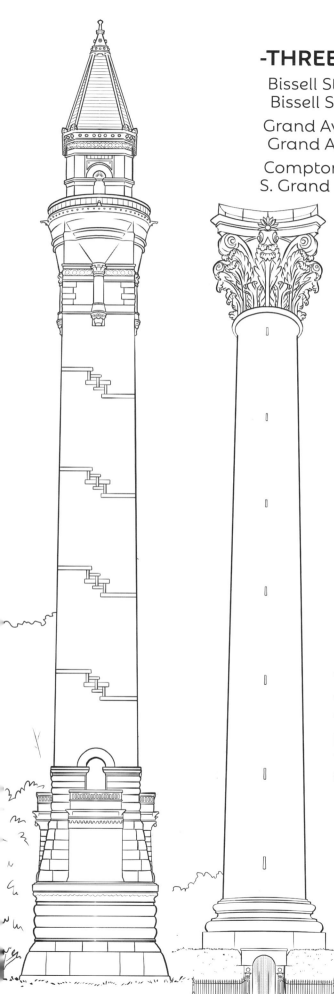

-THREE WATER TOWERS-

Bissell Street Water Tower, 1886
Bissell Street and Blair Avenue

Grand Avenue Water Tower, 1871
Grand Avenue and 20th Street

Compton Hill Water Tower, 1898
S. Grand and Russell boulevards

Unlike the bulb-shaped towers seen in small towns today, none of St. Louis's famous historic water towers ever held a reserve of water.

These were standpipe towers, once used to keep pressure steady in the city's vast plumbing network.

Without them, residents would have suffered weak trickles or explosive blasts from their faucets, firehoses, and street pumps.

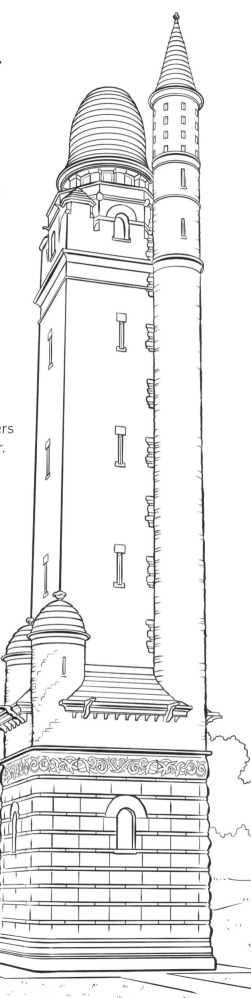

-TOWER GROVE PARK PAVILIONS-

Bounded by Magnolia Avenue, S. Grand Boulevard, Arsenal Street, and Kingshighway
Various architects, ca. 1870

Some of Tower Grove Park's most beloved features are its whimsical pavilions, which date back to the park's earliest years.

The Turkish Pavilion's onion-shaped dome once held roosts for pigeons and doves.

Henry Shaw donated the land for Tower Grove Park in 1868.

-MERCHANTS EXCHANGE BUILDING-
3rd and Chestnut streets
Francis Lee and Thomas Annan, 1875

Taking up a whole block of 3rd Street, the Merchants Exchange Building was where prices were set, contracts were signed, and investments were made on the river-front's countless tradeable goods.

The Italianate style featured oversize door and window details and monumental base-level blocks.

While the Merchants Exchange looked like one massive structure from street level, it was actually two U-shaped buildings. The enclosed trading hall sat between them. In 1875 it was the largest un-interrupted interior space in the country.

Because of changing technology and the clearance of the riverfront, the last day of trading closed on September 13, 1957. Despite protests, the landmark structure was demolished the next year.

-FLOUNDER HOUSE-
Old North, Soulard, Carondelet
Various architects, ca. 1870s–1900s

A flounder house has a roof that slopes in one direction, and its windows and doors are all situated on the same side.

Flounder houses were nicknamed after a type of fish that has all its features on one side of its body.

Legend says owners could claim a flounder house only had half a roof, and therefore they could pay fewer taxes. While it's a great story, no evidence for this claim has ever been found.

-LAFAYETTE SQUARE TOWNHOUSE-

Lafayette Square
Various architects, ca. 1870s–1880s

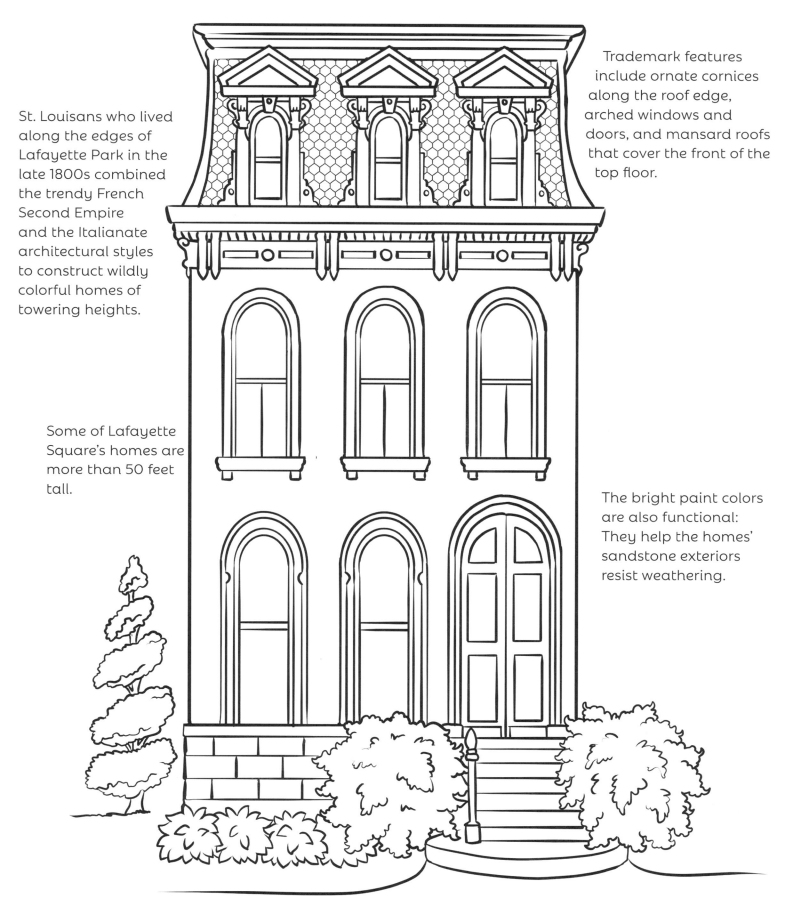

Trademark features include ornate cornices along the roof edge, arched windows and doors, and mansard roofs that cover the front of the top floor.

St. Louisans who lived along the edges of Lafayette Park in the late 1800s combined the trendy French Second Empire and the Italianate architectural styles to construct wildly colorful homes of towering heights.

Some of Lafayette Square's homes are more than 50 feet tall.

The bright paint colors are also functional: They help the homes' sandstone exteriors resist weathering.

-CUPPLES MANSION-
3673 W. Pine Boulevard
Thomas B. Annan, 1890

Built by woodenware industrialist Samuel Cupples, the castle-like Cupples Mansion cost more than $500,000 to build at a time when the average house cost about $3,000.

Mansions of this era typically had a third-floor ballroom, but Samuel Cupples disapproved of dancing.

The Cupples Mansion has 42 rooms and 22 fireplaces.

-WAINWRIGHT BUILDING-

111 N. 7th Street
Louis Sullivan, 1891

Chicago architect Louis Sullivan claimed that the Wainwright Building—designed for St. Louis brewer Ellis Wainwright—was where his vision for skyscrapers came together for the first time.

Sullivan modeled his skyscrapers on the sections of an ancient column: a plain base, a tall and repetitive shaft of floors, and a decorative capital.

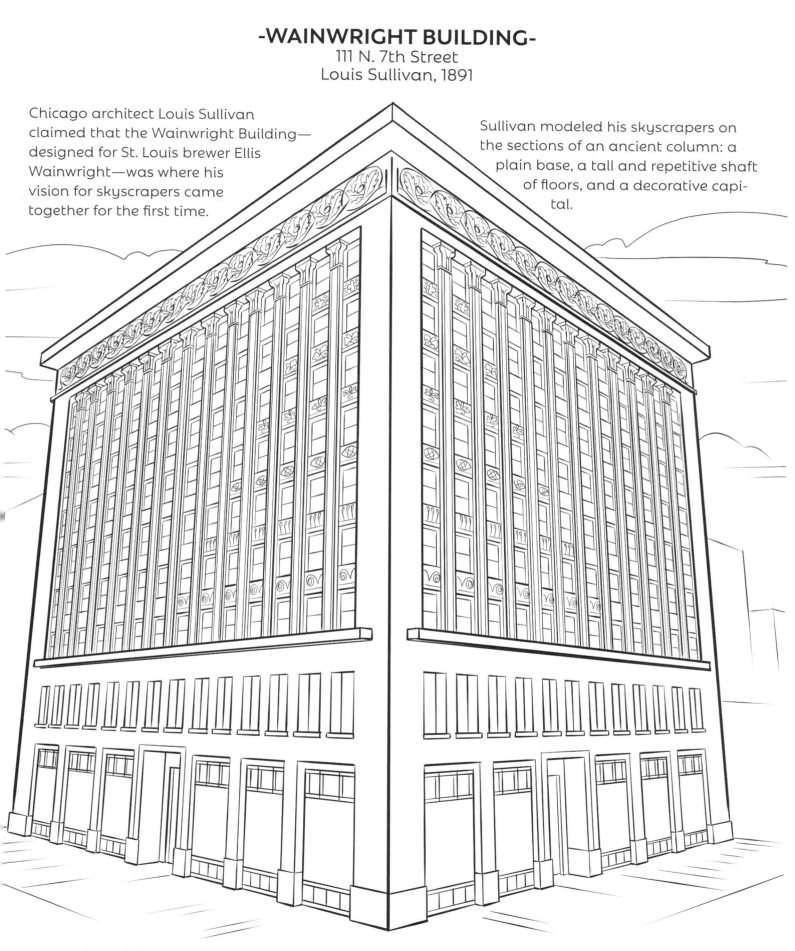

His buildings' ornamentation mixed intricate vegetation with geometric shapes.

-UNION STATION-
18th and Market streets
Theodore Link, 1894

Modeled after the 13th-century walled city of Carcassonne, France, Union Station was St. Louis's front door for millions of travelers.

Union Station's 230-foot clock tower holds a 30,000-gallon water tank that could be used in case of a fire.

During World War II it was among the busiest train stations in the world, moving 100,000 passengers per day.

Its 498,000-square-foot train shed covers more than six city blocks.

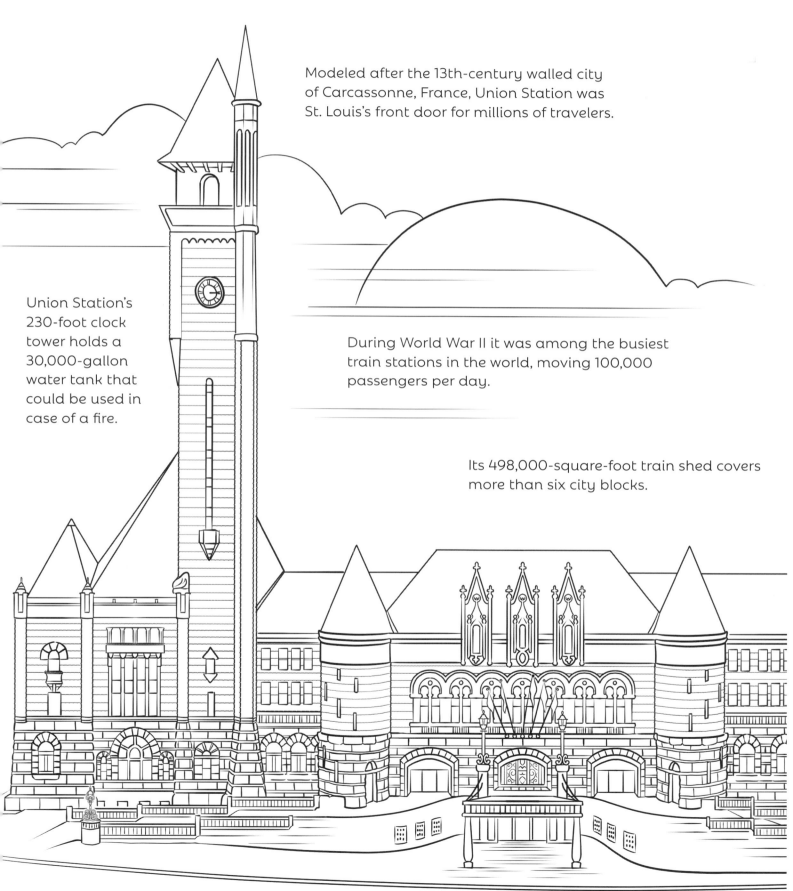

-URBAN ROWHOUSE-
Old North, Hyde Park, Soulard, Benton Park
Various architects, ca. 1890s

Between 1840 and 1900, St. Louis's population sky-rocketed from under 20,000 residents to more than half a million.

A rowhouse sometimes held 20 or more residents, with a different family living on each floor.

Block after block of tall, narrow rowhouses squeezed in between storefronts, factories, and churches, keeping everything nearby at a time when people walked everywhere.

A mousehole is a small, tunnel-like exterior passage-way that offers quick movement between the front and back of a house.

-ASHLEY STREET POWER HOUSE-

1220 Lewis Street
Charles Ledlie, 1903

This was once St. Louis's main source of power for everything from homes to electric streetcars to the 1904 World's Fair.

In the early 1900s it could consume 1,500 tons of coal every day—that's a pile of coal as big as a basketball court and 13 feet deep!

Busch Stadium, Union Station, the Gateway Arch, and more than 100 other downtown structures still rely on it for heat.

It feeds a 22-mile-long steam heat loop that courses beneath downtown St. Louis.

-UNIVERSITY CITY'S CITY HALL-
6801 Delmar Boulevard
Herbert Chivers, 1903

In 1902, *Woman's Magazine* publisher Edward Gardner Lewis began assembling land on St. Louis's outskirts for a model city, dedicated to knowledge and the arts. At the center of "University City" would be a circular plaza ringed with monumental structures, beginning with the octagonal, five-story Magazine Building that housed his publishing empire.

Its dome houses a retractable 80-inch-wide searchlight. In 1904 it was reportedly the most powerful one in the world.

In 1910, Lewis declared bankruptcy. The Magazine Building was rededicated as the city hall of University City in 1930.

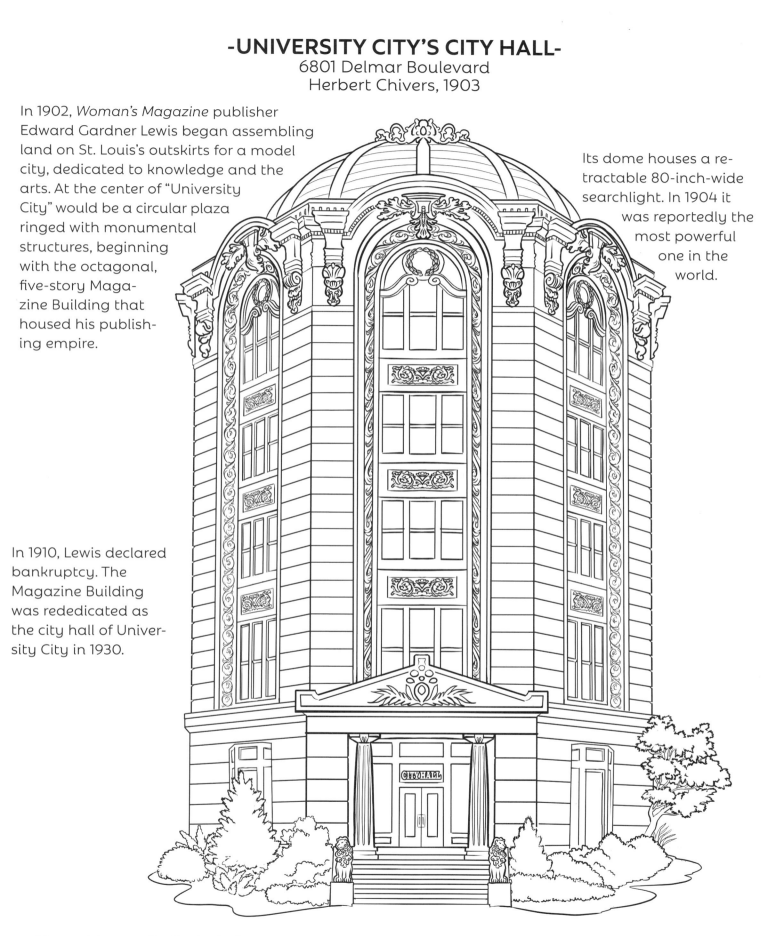

Named for an elite Paris design school, the Beaux-Arts style took classical architecture's symmetry and covered it with statues, flowers, garlands, and ornaments.

-MCKINLEY HIGH SCHOOL-
2156 Russell Boulevard
William B. Ittner, 1904

St. Louis architect William B. Ittner revolutionized school design by reimagining small, cold, dark school buildings as daylight-filled castles.

McKinley's terra-cotta entrance contains symbolic occupational shields of doctors, blacksmiths, painters, and more.

Throughout his career Ittner designed more than 430 schools across the nation. Yeatman and McKinley were his first two high schools.

Ittner's schools included then-uncommon spaces, such as playgrounds, gymnasiums, and science laboratories.

-FESTIVAL HALL-
Art Hill in Forest Park
Cass Gilbert, 1904

Festival Hall towered over the grounds of the 1904 World's Fair. Despite its monumental size and majestic appearance, Festival Hall was built mostly out of temporary materials. It was only meant to last as long as the Fair.

A waterfall called the "Cascades" spilled out of it and into the Grand Basin below. The Cascades produced 45,000 gallons of water a minute.

Inside was a 3,500-seat auditorium and the world's largest pipe organ.

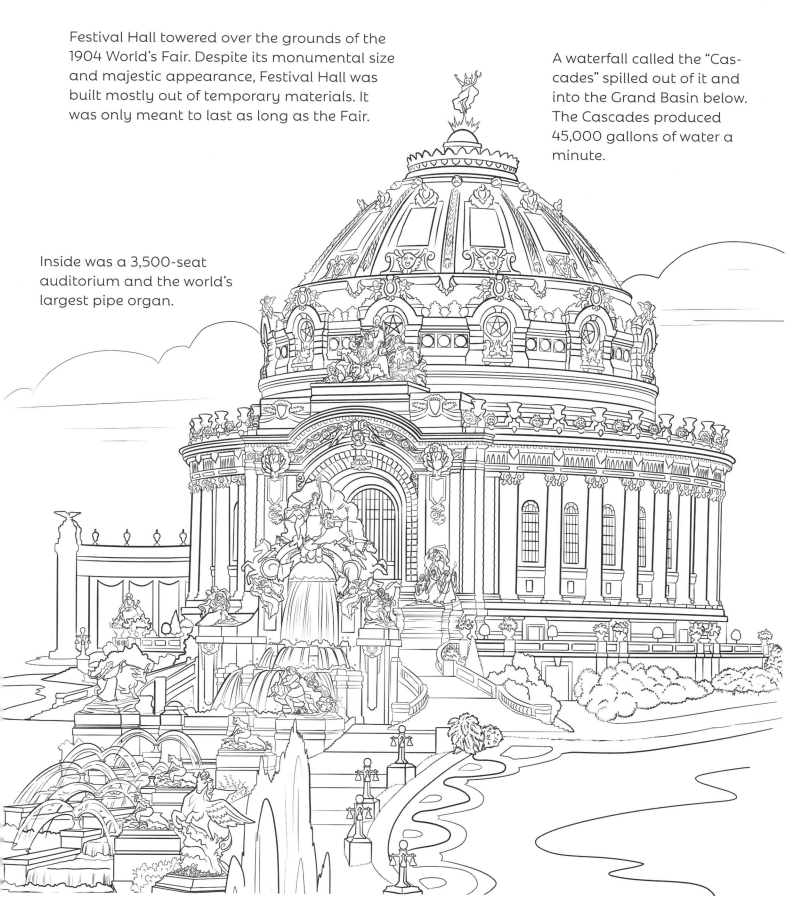

-SHOTGUN HOUSE-
Bevo, the Hill, the Ville, Walnut Park, East St. Louis
Various architects, ca. 1900s

Typically composed of a living room, kitchen, and bedroom all lined up in a row, the "shotgun" nickname refers to either the house's gun-barrel shape or the idea that you could fire a gun straight through it without hitting any walls.

Some shotgun homes measure less than 600 square feet and are barely 12 feet wide.

In 1910 a shotgun house on the Hill cost about $1,000.

-TWO-FAMILY FLAT-
St. Louis city and inner suburbs
Various architects, ca. 1910s

Lining streets from Carondelet to University City to Baden, few building styles have shaped St. Louis's urban culture more than the two-family flat.

The top edge of the front wall, called a parapet, is often ornately decorated.

These residences look like a single home but have two front doors that lead to separate apartments on each floor.

Two-family flats provide owners with a built-in source of income, and sometimes extended families share one.

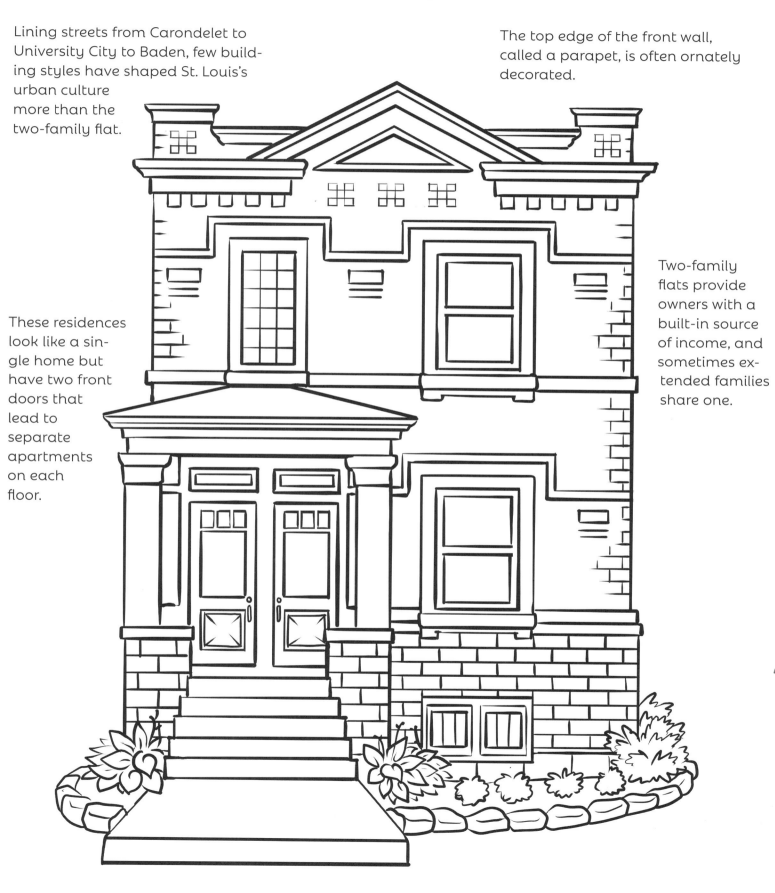

-LEMP BREWERY-
Lemp Avenue and Cherokee Street
Various architects, ca. 1874–1911

A fleet of 500 refrigerated railcars carried Lemp beer from coast to coast.

Built above a natural cave system that was perfect for storing lager, Lemp was St. Louis's largest brewery by the 1870s.

Lemp's brewing empire fell flat once Prohibition made alcohol illegal in the United States in 1919. In 1922 the International Shoe Company bought the Lemp Brewery complex for a fraction of its pre-Prohibition value.

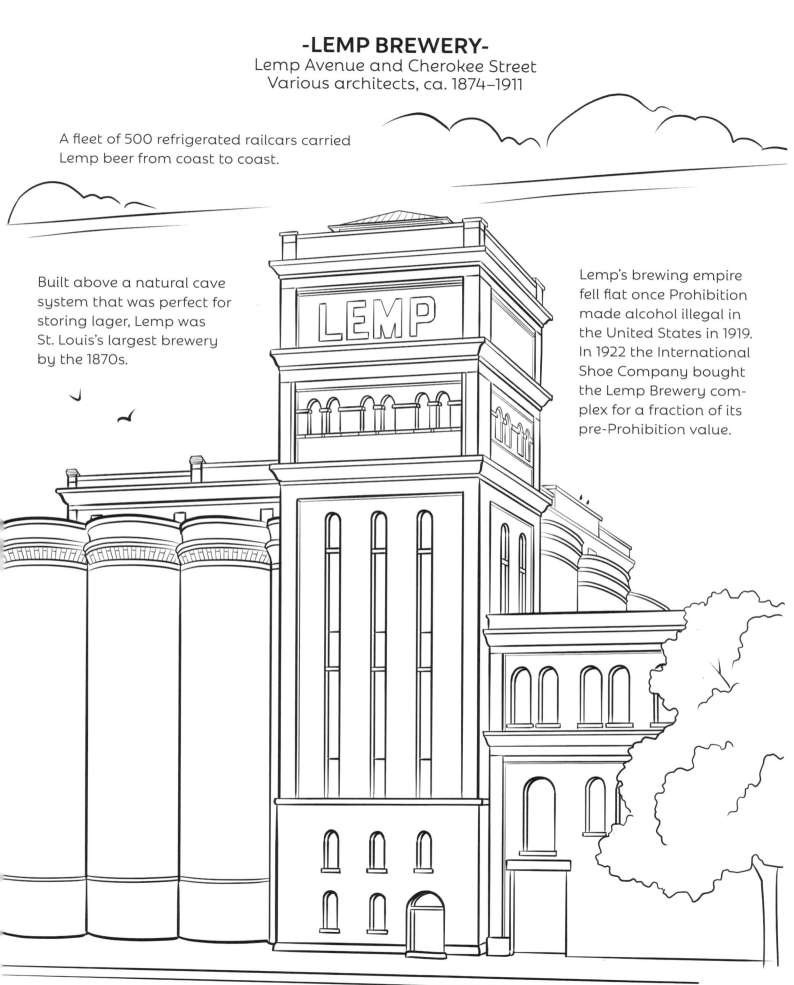

-CATHEDRAL BASILICA OF SAINT LOUIS-
4431 Lindell Boulevard
Barnett, Haynes & Barnett, 1908–1914

Built as a much-needed upgrade from the comparably small "Old Cathedral" on the riverfront, the enormous "New Cathedral" has a grandeur that few other religious structures can match.

It was designated a basilica—a church of distinguished importance—by Pope John Paul II in 1997.

The interior's glimmering walls and ceilings are covered in more than 41 million pieces of mosaic glass in over 7,000 colors. Installing it all took 76 years.

Inside, sounds echo for nearly seven seconds.

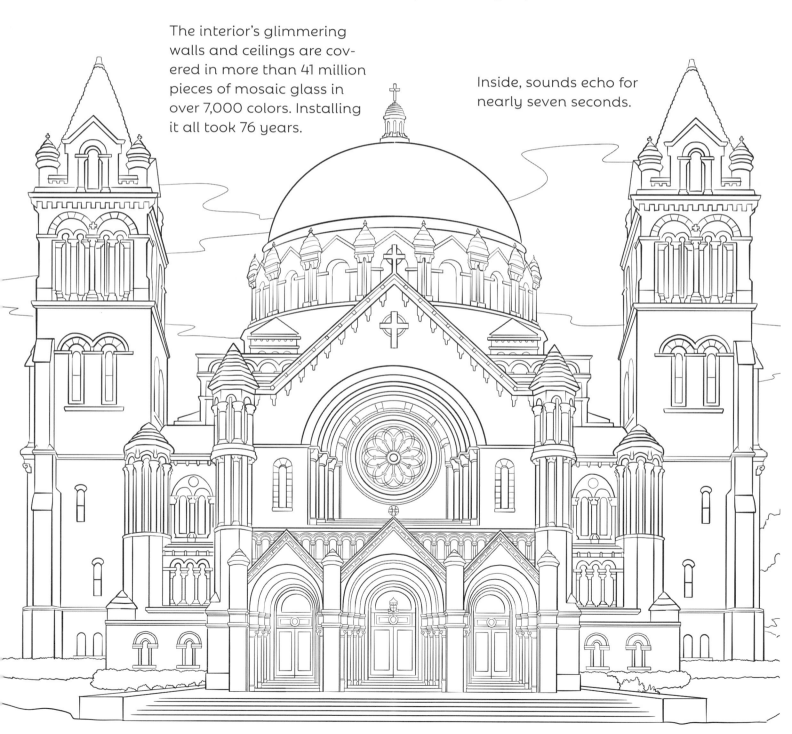

-BEVO MILL-
4749 Gravois Avenue
Klipstein & Rathmann, 1917

The windmill contains a three-story apartment; celebrity chef Henry Dietz once lived there.

After growing calls for the prohibition of alcohol, Anheuser-Busch built a series of charming Old World taverns to try and convince the public that beer was a safe—and even necessary—ingredient of a healthy society.

Complete with a whirling windmill and roaring fireplace, Bevo Mill was the opposite of the average saloon.

The mill's 4-foot-thick base is built of limestone pulled from Grant's Farm.

-FOX THEATRE-
527 N. Grand Boulevard
C. Howard Crane, 1929

The most extravagant movie palace of 1920s St. Louis, the Fox Theatre offered showgoers a fantasy escape.

The Great Depression rocked America just months after the Fox opened, and theaters this opulent would never rise again.

Wildlife depicted in the Fox Theatre's terra-cotta façade includes owls, rams, snakes, and exotic birds.

With 5,060 seats, it was once the third-largest theater in the country.

-ST. LOUIS ARENA-
5700 Oakland Avenue
Gustel Kiewitt, 1929

Built in 1929 as a venue for live-stock exhibitions, the Arena was best known as the original home of the St. Louis Blues hockey team from 1967 to 1993.

The Arena was also used by professional basketball's St. Louis Hawks (1955–1968) and Spirits of St. Louis (1974–1976), as well as professional soccer's St. Louis Steamers (1979–1988) and St. Louis Ambush (1992–1994).

St. Louisans watched as the Arena was imploded live on television on February 27, 1999.

A 12-story building could have stood at center ice and still cleared the Arena's roof.

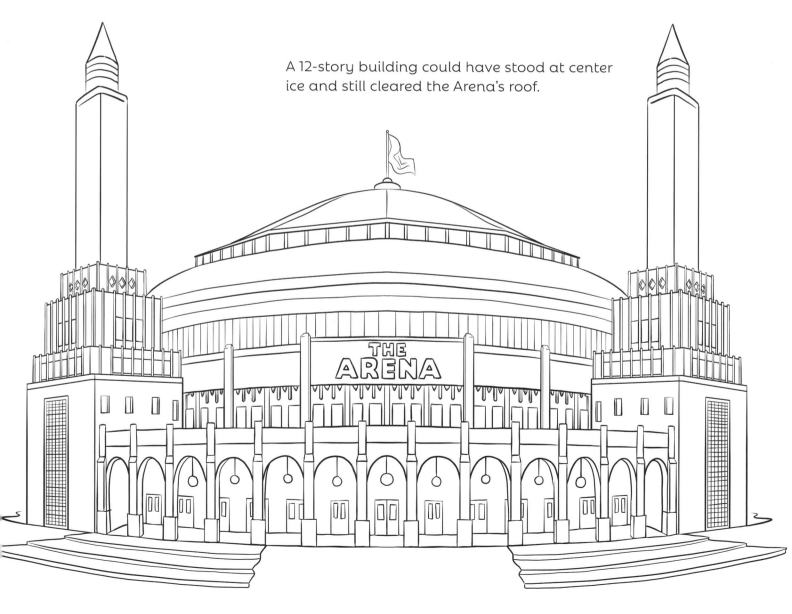

-SOULARD MARKET-
730 Carroll Street
Albert Osburg, 1929

The current market building—the second to stand there—was modeled after Filippo Brunelleschi's Foundling Hospital, built in 1419 in Florence, Italy.

At nearly 650 feet long, Soulard Market is longer than the span of the Arch's legs.

The second floor contains a full-size basketball court and a theater stage.

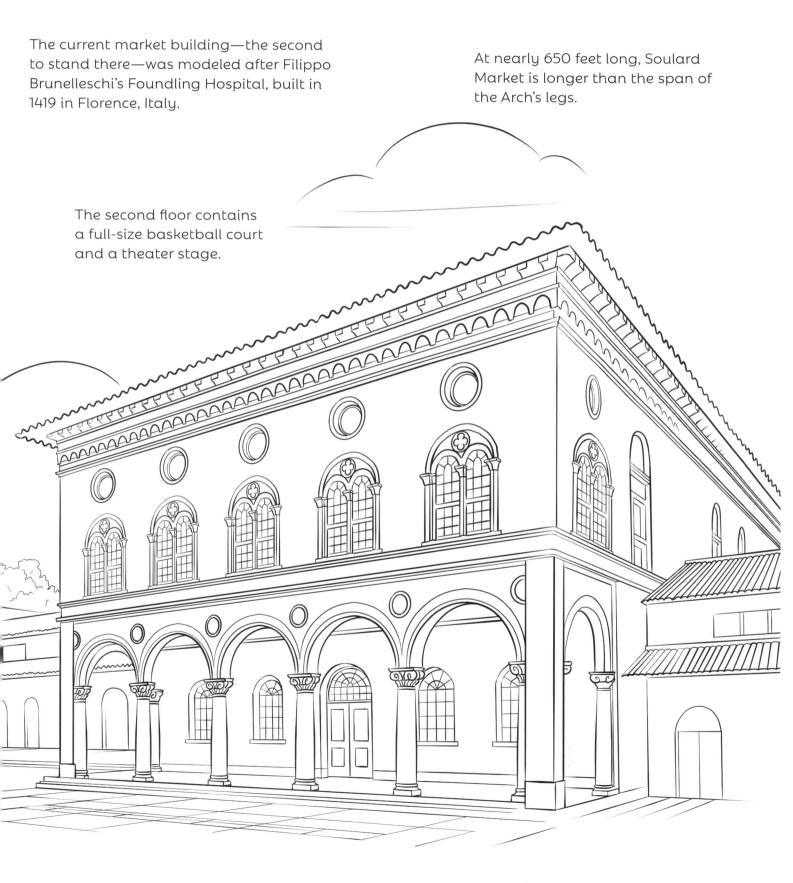

-HOMER G. PHILLIPS HOSPITAL-
2601 Whittier Street
Albert Osburg, 1937

St. Louis's Black citizens had lacked reliable access to a hospital until local lawyer and activist Homer G. Phillips bargained with St. Louis mayor Henry Kiel to get one funded.

By the late 1940s one-third of the country's Black medical graduates had studied there.

With 685 beds, Homer G. Phillips was one of the 10 largest general-practice hospitals in the United States in 1937.

Completed in 1937, Homer G. Phillips Hospital was among the country's first training centers for Black doctors and a centerpiece of the Ville neighborhood.

-GINGERBREAD HOUSE-

Affton, Southampton, Richmond Heights, Jennings, Baden
Various architects, ca. 1930s–1940s

Gingerbreads are nicknamed for their resemblance to
the holiday season's candy-covered treats.

St. Louis's gingerbread
houses are frosted with
rough stones, arched door-
ways, heavy timber, pastel
stained glass, and oversize
chimneys.

The steep, curving portion
of roof that plunges down-
ward is called a catslide.

Influences recall Gothic Revival, Tudor
Revival, and art deco styles.

-CORAL COURT MOTEL-
7755 Watson Road
Adolph Struebig and Harold Tyrer, 1941–1946

With "built for speed" curves and glisten-
ing tile, the Coral Court Motel was one of
St. Louis's slickest spots for travelers to
stay during the heyday of Route 66.

Preservationists and fans rallied to
save the "no-tell motel," but it was demolished for a housing tract in 1995.

Later, discrete garages,
hourly rental options, and
privacy-providing glass-
block windows made the
Coral Court perfect for any
no-questions-asked use
you could think of.

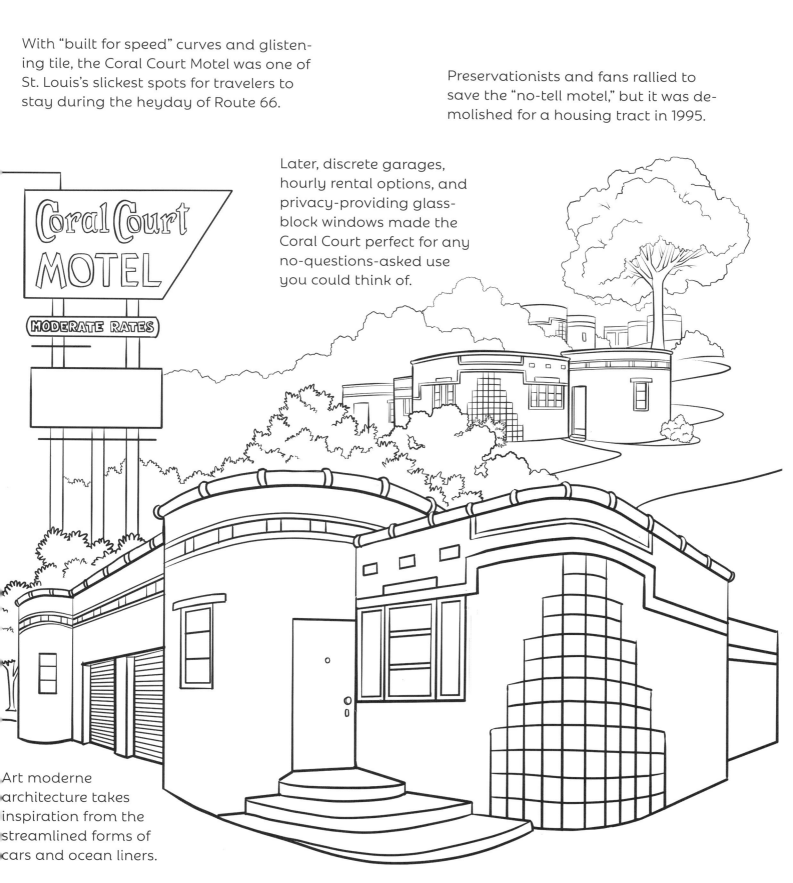

Art moderne
architecture takes
inspiration from the
streamlined forms of
cars and ocean liners.

-CITY MUSEUM-
750 N. 16th Street
Bob and Gail Cassilly, 1997

Built of repurposed industrial debris and lots of imagination, the City Museum turned a 600,000-square-foot former shoe factory into an urban wonderland that defies definition.

Since its 1997 opening, the City Museum has grown like a living organism, spreading onto the front of the building and even onto its roof.

The rooftop's praying mantis weighs 3,000 pounds.

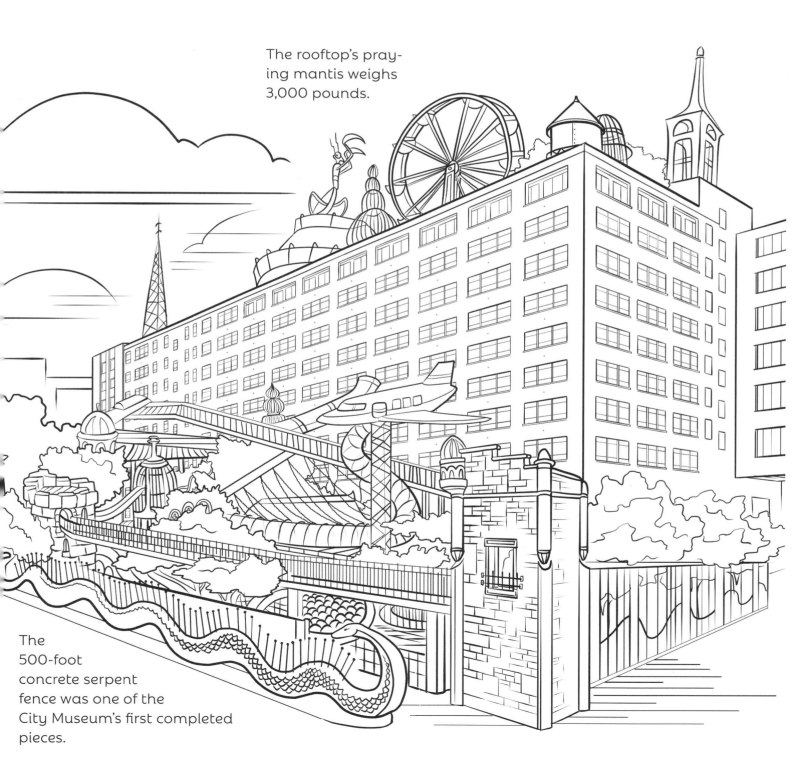

The 500-foot concrete serpent fence was one of the City Museum's first completed pieces.

-ONE HUNDRED-
100 N. Kingshighway
Studio Gang, 2020

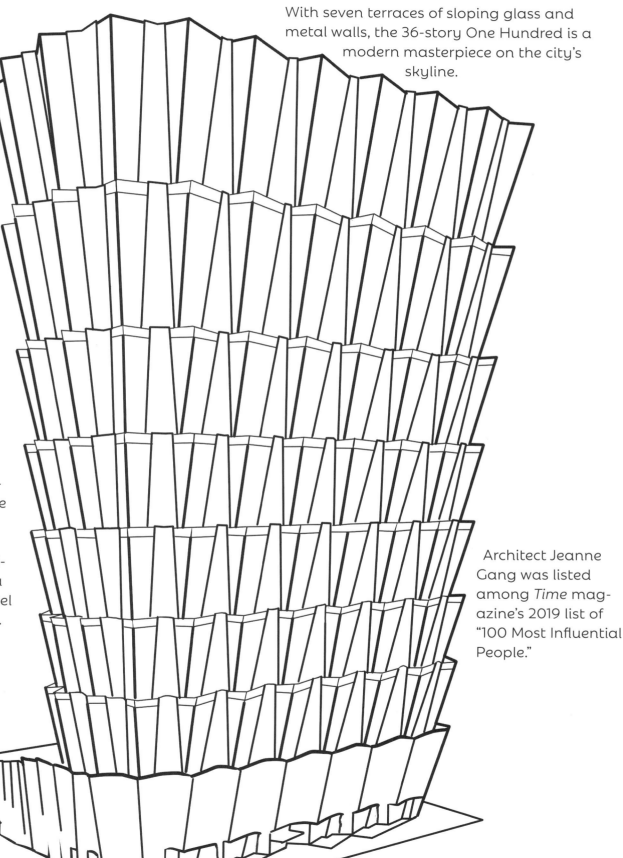

With seven terraces of sloping glass and metal walls, the 36-story One Hundred is a modern masterpiece on the city's skyline.

Each of the 316 apartments has a corner made entirely of floor-to-ceiling windows.

The building combines cutting-edge design with nods to nearby historic landmarks, including the Park Plaza tower and the Jewel Box in Forest Park.

Architect Jeanne Gang was listed among *Time* magazine's 2019 list of "100 Most Influential People."